MATTHEW D. HUTCHESON

Patriot in Prison

Capitalism v Socialism

Excerpt
Chapter 14

This book resides in the following BISAAC Categories:

- Nonfiction > Political Science > History & Theory
- Nonfiction > Political Science > Comparative Politics

BelloHutch

For more about Matthew D. Hutcheson, and other writings, visit www.bellohutch.com

In Latin, "Bello" means "fight for."
BelloHutch@gmail.com

AreULost Press

For more information:

info@areulost.org

FOREWORD to Matthew Hutcheson's
Capitalism vs. Socialism

Recently on social media the question was asked, "Would you rather have Freedom or Security?" I was shocked and saddened that so many answered "Security," not realizing that it is Freedom which gives them Security. Giving up your Freedom makes you vulnerable to other people's desires and decisions. You no longer have a say in what you can and cannot do. Benjamin Franklin said,

"Any society that will give up a little liberty to gain a little security will deserve neither and lose both."

While reading this book, you will learn that Capitalism is true Freedom and is the reason that it always wins in the end. You will learn the elements of Capitalism and how to think and how to make educated decisions about what Freedom truly is and more importantly, how to keep it.

Today's attacks on Capitalism by the new "Progressives" must stop. Giving up our Freedoms to false idolatries like the "Green New Deal" or "Medicare for all" will never stand the test of time and is absolutely not what the Framers of the Constitution desired for this nation. We were founded on hard work, the deep love of God and Country, and Courage.

The Courage shown by Matt in writing this book in the worst possible conditions, after having his government turn on him and imprison him in terrible conditions, is rarely seen in today's society. Yet, Matt has never faltered in his love of God or Country.

Please settle in and enjoy this great passage on the living foundations of this blessed nation. Share it with your family, share it with your friends. As President Ronald Reagan so eloquently stated,

> *"Freedom is never more than one generation away from extinction. We didn't pass it to our children in the bloodstream. It must be fought for, protected, and handed on for them to do the same."*

Annette Hutcheson

Contents

Patriot in Prison

The pages you are about to read were written by a federal prisoner, **Matthew D. Hutcheson**, under the extreme conditions of solitary confinement sometime between November 16, 2015 and March 24, 2016. It was written by pen and paper, without source materials, and transcribed by his mother. It memorializes a five-week prison sponsored class at FCI Terminal Island, California. The class was intended to be about entrepreneurialism, but instead evolved into a political discussion on freedom, socialism, capitalism and more. Prepare to be inspired and informed. This prisoner-sourced document, soon to be published as part of a book titled, "**Patriot in Prison**," will be one of the most important explanations of liberty and America you will ever read.

Respectfully Submitted,

Jerry L. Melchisedeck, Sr., Lt Col USAF (Ret).
Jay Inman, Lt Col US Army (Ret).
Robert Gilbeau, Fmr. Rear Admiral US Navy (Ret).
Lee Ofner, DDS
John Jenkins, JD

Capitalism Vs. Socialism

Find these articles and other resources at:

<http://bellohutch.com/>

- o <u>An Unlikely American Hero Has Emerged From An Even More Unlikely Place=Prison</u>
- o <u>Is America's Greatest Citizen A Prisoner?</u>

- o <u>Whatever Happened to Matt Hutcheson – Part 1</u>
- o <u>Matthew D Hutcheson for President? What the World Has to Say</u>
- o <u>Independence Day 2019 – In Defense of America</u>

- o <u>The American Hypothesis</u>

Matt Hutcheson is REAL! The following pictures and introduction will move Matt from Theory to Practical in the reader's mind.

Testifying Before Congress 2007

Capitalism Vs. Socialism

Creating Greater Accounting Transparency for Pensioners: Matthew Hutcheson

Testifying Before Congress 2010

Many incidents of violence occur because of desperation. Such desperation is caused not only by economic disparities, but also because individuals have not been taught correct principles. Economic disparities are caused by a lack of trust in societal ideas and by refusal to apply those ideas which successful people accept as given. Do not just give a guy a principle; teach him how to live it and he will be free for a lifetime.

I came to these observations after I was asked by the psychology department at the prison to teach an entrepreneurial class to the students of a Residential Drug Addiction Program or RDAP. Every race was represented in the class.

This class provided a safe environment for inmates to ask questions and fascinating discussions were had. A discussion about entrepreneurialism cannot be had without an understanding of free trade and markets. The notion that a person can create capital from the production or invention of goods and services, which can be reinvested to produce more capital, is the single greatest human invention. Albert Einstein has called the greatest human invention "compound interest." That statement is a fun saying to repeat, but Einstein was incorrect. The greatest discovery is capitalism—the source of compound interest. Capitalism is not created. It is naturally occurring, and therefore can only be discovered.

During the first class, I saw first-hand how intelligent these men were and how they starved for knowledge and understanding. Following are recaps of the classes which I taught to the best of my memory. I love teaching with the question and answer method.

Week #1 Entrepreneurial Class - Capitalism

"Where did capitalism come from?" one classmate asked.

"It was discovered, not created," I said. "Ideas or objects that are discovered are part of nature or are part of the natural occurrence of things."

"How was it discovered?"

"There are many different examples," I explained. "The discovery was so normal to the observer that he probably did not even recognize it as a discovery. Take livestock for example. Let us say you own a cow which eventually bears a calf. Once you had one asset (the cow). Now you have two. Your original asset (capital) has doubled itself."

"But it didn't just happen. There was effort involved, wasn't there?" asked another classmate.

"Of course, effort and work are always part of the success equation."

The classmate was understanding it. One said, "If the rancher bred the cow and also the calf, he would then have four animals."

"Right, and do not forget the value goes beyond breeding. Milk can be sold for income."

"So," said the inmate, "Someone can own a valuable asset and also earn income from it without diminishing the value of the asset."

"Right."

Another inmate chimed in. "It's just like a rental house."

"Precisely," I said. "Thousands of years ago, humans discovered they could obtain revenue or income from their property. Sheep produce sheerings of wool to sell. Buildings could be used as inns. Horses and camels could be rented out for transportation, oxen for field work."

"You're saying that wealth is tied to income producing capital?"

"Correct."

"And that is what a capitalist is?"

"Right. A capitalist is someone who lives on the income produced from assets he owns."

"What's so bad about that? That's exactly what we all want," exclaimed a class member.

"It's not bad. It's good," recognized another.

"Then why have we always been told that capitalists are evil?" asked still another.

"Who told you that?"

"I dunno. No particular person. Maybe politicians. It's just a belief we all have."

All heads were nodding, and classmates made comments to each other. I asked for clarification. "Yet you guys want to be entrepreneurs, which is good. Entrepreneurs are the life blood of capitalism."

"Then capitalism is not evil," one inmate said with new understanding.

"Perhaps you are wondering where the false idea that 'capitalism is evil' crept into the narrative of society?" They nodded. "Capitalism is a way for an individual to realize his or her full potential. It is true that multiple individuals may partner up in an endeavor, but the main objective is a favorable outcome for each individual."

"That's where work and effort come in?"

"In part, yes. A successful capitalist has three core things going for him or her. First is knowledge of the income-producing asset, including an understanding of, and relationship with, buyers for the goods or services offered. It requires study, and the ability to build and maintain relationships of trust with customers or clients."

"So a capitalist should be a trusted member of society."

"Yes, ideally. At a minimum, trust needs to exist between buyers and sellers. The second thing is a knowledge and understanding of risk and how to manage it."

"Like what to do if all your sheep get sick and die!" one said.

"Right," I said, "and how to prevent it."

"Cool! And the third?" they asked.

"The third is the ability to persevere in the face of great obstacles, adversity, or loss. Being a capitalist takes great courage. Without courageous capitalists, there would be no cars, no cell phones, no airplanes, no electronics, no grocery stores, no modern medicine, no new knowledge, or new methods. The list goes on and on. Without free trade and capitalism, we would be walking everywhere we went, growing our own food, and making our own clothes."

Capitalism Vs. Socialism

"Without capitalism, the prison system would not be bursting at the seams with human warehousing." All laughed, but it was a sad laugh.

"Unfortunately, it is true. It is one reason some dislike or distrust capitalism. When someone's capital consists of human beings behind bars, profit derived from human suffering can be viewed as evil. But guys, we should not let what the government has done to us infect our belief system about capitalism."

One inmate spoke up. "Like anything, evil can creep into the good."

"Thank you for bringing us back on point," I said. "The purity of capitalism can be corrupted by individuals or by governments who have too much influence over free trade. Kings can lay claim to an individual's capital, illegally encroaching on a person's ownership rights. Governments can over-tax or over-regulate. In my personal case, a governmental agency encroached on a private endeavor by which it felt threatened, and thus tried to destroy the endeavor by incarcerating me. Other individuals can corrupt pure capitalism by introducing force or fraud into a transaction."

"Like the Mafia?" one inmate posed.

"Exactly," I said. "When fraud, force, deception, or encroachment interferes with free trade, capitalism begins to fail."

One astute inmate asked, "Did I understand you correctly that capitalism is at risk by unchecked power, whether by a king, government, by force or fraud, by anyone?"

"Yes, you understood correctly. When capitalism fails, things can become quite scary. It leaves the populace open to encroaching forms of government in which freedom can be lost."

"What kinds of government?" someone asked.

"Monarchies, socialism, communism, totalitarianism."

"Like Hitler?"

"Yes, and many others that came before him"

"Could a government like Hitler ever happen again?"

"It could."

"How can we prevent it?"

"That question reveals the growing seed of knowledge and wisdom developing inside each of you," I told the class. "Remember, capitalism is not government. Rather, capitalism is simply the naturally occurring multiplication of assets and generation of income within a free society. Once that freedom to grow and expand is destroyed by other influences, whatever they may be, a form of government will emerge which will seek to control or oppress the naturally occurring. The idea of something being 'naturally occurring' was referred to by the Founding Fathers as 'self-evident.'"

"I can see how our government interferes with capitalism," one said in a discouraging tone. The class was silent, thinking.

I ended the class by saying, "next week I will share a history lesson about our nation, about capitalism, and how each of us can be part of the solution to preserve freedom and liberty for our children and grandchildren."

Capitalism Vs. Socialism

One student teased, "Hey man, talking about freedom and liberty is a sore point with us." The group broke out in laughter. I could not hold back a hardly laugh either. "See you next week."

Week #2 Entrepreneurial Class - History

"Good to see you guys again. Do you have any questions from last week's class?"

Eager to continue, the class asked me to start where I left off. These men looked at me with a focus that created a near-palpable feeling in the room. They waited as if I were about to unfold the greatest mystery of life to them for the first time. The environment was electric in anticipation of what I had to say that day. I began.

"Remember, last time I said government's purpose is to protect the naturally occurring from encroachment by others, including itself."

"What did you say, 'naturally occurring' meant again?" one student asked.

"It means self-evident rights given to us by a power greater than man's power and an authority greater than man's authority. Here is an example. Each of you has talents. When you develop your talents and abilities, you are happy. You have the right to pursue happiness. The government is supposed to protect your right to pursue the development of your talents, interests, entrepreneurial ventures, acquisition of assets and income, and so on. As long as you do not encroach on others in your pursuit of happiness, the government's primary purpose is to ensure that the interests of others, or even the government itself, does not encroach on you. The government is also there to protect our lives from those who would do us harm, whether in or out of the United States. It is also there to preserve our liberty from those who would take it from us."

Another inmate said, "Where did the phrase 'Life, liberty, and the pursuit of happiness' come from?"

An inmate from the back row piped up and said, "The Declaration of Independence, you dummy."

"Please do not call him 'dummy.'"

"Sorry."

"It is a better question than you might think. Really, a very good question. Actually, most people do not understand how that phrase appeared in the Declaration of Independence. I would like to take you on a little historical journey."

The entire class sat up and leaned forward in anticipation. I began by explaining conditions thousands of years ago.

"Families were organized into societal bodies which today we call tribes. Families obeyed tribal rules. Disputes were settled within the tribes. Different tribes might fight with each other from time to time, but by and large, peace and capitalism prevailed. Over time, tribes began to appoint kings, believing that a king would make their lives better. The opposite happened. More wars were fought, and freedoms lost.

"Eventually, even ancient Israel demanded a human king over their Heavenly King. Centuries of suffering, bloodshed, and loss of liberty was the result.

"When the Founding Fathers declared *'all men are created equal,'* they intentionally took a swipe at the legitimacy of the King of Great Britain. They essentially stated that he was no longer king over them, and that they now were going to form a government which ensured the individual's '*life, liberty, and pursuit of happiness*.' Do you value your lives?"

"What kind of question is that?" one asked.

I responded, "I take it as a 'yes'?!"

"Yes."

"Do you value liberty?"

"More than you know," retorted a student.

Everybody laughed.

"Do not forget," I said, "I am in here just like you, and I do know how much you value liberty."

"Oh yeah, sometimes we forget you are a prisoner, too."

"Do you value happiness?"

"Of course," they said.

"If our government drifts from its purpose of ensuring the rights of life, liberty, and the pursuit of happiness, then we can be sure that a new form of government will soon be found on the doorstep knocking. Never ever take the miracle of America for granted."

I explained that liberty and capitalism are naturally occurring, absent the "pride of kings" as Thomas Paine put it. Since happiness means different things to different people, each person's unique flavor of happiness must be chosen by the individual. I explained that this important phrase in the Declaration is the result of centuries of thinking and debating of great human minds. The debate found moments of success, one particularly worth mentioning. It was when King John of England signed the Magna Carta June 15, 1215.

"What's the Magna Carta?" one asked.

"The Magna Carta was a governing document that placed checks and balances on the king. Essentially the new document declared 'The King is not King. The Law is King.' Magna Carta is Latin for 'great charter' or 'grand governing law.' The Magna Carta created the first concept of co-equal branches of government, similar to our Executive branch, the President; Legislative branch, Congress; and the Judicial branch, the courts. However, as good a step forward as the Magna Carta was, three problems lingered on with England's form of government.

"First, England kept the monarchial form of government—that is, kings and queens— who sometimes ruled in monarchial tyranny.

"Second, England had a class system which was also a form of tyranny, often referred to as 'Aristocratical Tyranny' which oppressed those with less money and clout.

"Third, was the common people who tried, often futilely, to insist the first two behave with moral virtue."

A hand was raised. "I have a question," said one member of the class. "I'm having trouble following all of this. Why are you telling us all this England stuff? It doesn't have anything to do with us today."

"I am thankful for your question. This history lesson is critically important information for you to understand. It sets the stage for some of the greatest events in human history. Please bear with me a little longer."

"Okay...I'm just sayin'."

"I understand. Hang with me, okay?"

"Okay."

"The colonists had reached some conclusions. First, if the king had to be checked by the common people, why have a king at all? Second, the king had very little information about the daily lives of the common people, yet the king was required to act in cases affecting people when the highest judgment was required. He often made very bad decisions.

"This situation presented a contradiction. The life of a king necessarily shuts him away from his subjects for self-protection, yet the business of a king required him to know the situation involving his subjects and to make decisions accordingly. Sometimes, the decisions made by the king were really encroachments. This contradiction, as pointed out by Thomas Paine, showed the colonists that being governed by a man across the ocean was ridiculous. Being subject to a local government 'for the people and by the people' was the only logical approach."

"So are you saying the colonists saw the king as someone who thought he was better than everybody else, but didn't know anything about them?"

"Correct. This kingly neglect evolved into oppression. The oppression evolved into violence. Casting off the king's claim on the colonies would require severing ties with England, which caused more violence."

"So, those guys just got together and wrote the Declaration of Independence one day?"

"Not even close. Let us finish this discussion next week."

After class that day I started thinking about a book I had read called *Way of the Kings* by Brandon Sanderson. Sanderson said:

"Often I wonder if my experiences in life—my easy life and my current level of comfort—have given me any true experience to use in making laws. If we had to rely on what we knew, kings would only be of use in creating laws regarding proper heating of tea and cushioning of thrones."

Such were the colonists' experiences. Do our government leaders today really understand the people they represent?

Week #3 Entrepreneurial Class - People

Francis Hutcheson, Adam Smith, Thomas Paine, John Locke and Thomas Jefferson

"Welcome back, guys," I began. To begin, I want to briefly review what we discussed during the prior two classes."

A Polynesian student interrupted, "Hutch, before you start could I ask you a question? In our first class we discussed natural occurrences...things that are self-evident. Is capitalism one of the natural occurrences?"

"Exactly. Go on."

"It dawned on me what you were saying. Like if this class was stranded on an island, capitalism would emerge naturally, automatically, right?"

I nodded and he continued. "I thought one of us might start harvesting coconuts. Another person might gather thatch for shelters. Another might catch fish. Another might dig roots. Someone might weave hammocks. Then at some point, we would start trading or bartering with each other to get things we need that the other person has. And whatever product has the greatest demand will get the greatest exchange."

"Bingo!" I exclaimed. "Beautifully stated."

"Aw thanks. This picture in my mind helped me understand why capitalism and free trade are self-evident. If some government suddenly started to interfere with our growing fragile economy, the entire process would fall apart. We could starve or die from exposure. I finally get it, I mean, why protecting capitalism is so crucial to society's well-being."

"I could not have stated it better myself. Your brilliant summary is basically what I wanted to cover for Week One. Now let me ask you a question. What if one of you on the island had nothing to offer because you lacked skills, knowledge, initiative, or all three? Say that one went from person to person asking each of you to give something to him of what you have worked so hard to accumulate through effort or trade when he has done nothing. How would you deal with such person?"

"We'd kick him off the island."

All laughed and nodded.

"Seriously," I said. "Let us say he is starving. What would you really do? Take a moment and think seriously about it."

After a period of pondering and contemplation, a hand raised.

"Go ahead."

"We'd have to form a committee or appoint a decision maker to decide how to deal with him."

"You have just formed a government," I said.

"Oh great." There was a round of laughter.

"At a minimum you have elected a judge. Now, let us say the judge says each of you will take a portion of your property to give to support the one without anything to offer."

"That sounds like a tax on us. We hope it would be fair," said one inmate.

Another inmate said, "Wouldn't it be better to teach him a trade or skills so he can be part of us without taking our stuff?"

"Excellent analysis. You are absolutely correct. As your society grows, you may find some who just cannot provide for themselves. In such cases, would you prefer to help support that individual of your own free will and choice, or do you want the judge to mandate how much you have to give?"

"On our own, for sure!"

"But what if your elected judge demands that you pay a tax. Then he creates a bunch of little technical rules making it increasingly difficult to provide for yourself, let alone for those who truly cannot take care of themselves? What then?"

"We would have to make big changes to our government. But wait! Can we do that?"

"You created the government to solve a problem. It was created by you to help you."

"So we can change the government?"

"Of course. You may have to define its parameters and authorities more narrowly. You have the power to control the government you created. It should never control you. Government is meant to prevent problems, not to be the problems.

"Remember last week I explained how government can and often does encroach on our rights instead of protecting them? It is particularly true with a king. I also explained how the colonists had arrived at the conclusion that the King of England was not what they wanted nor that to which they were entitled. But this conclusion did not happen overnight. The seeds were planted in the 1215 Magna Carta. Those seeds continued to grow very slowly into the late 1600's. Remember, last week I told you the idea of 'Life, Liberty, and the pursuit of happiness' was the result of centuries of thinking and debating of great human minds. In the late 1600's and early 1700's there was a burst of human enlightenment with respect to the rights that God gives us, rights that did not come from a king or government. Making such a discovery was dangerous back then."

"It still is!" one class member exclaimed. The class chuckled and nodded.

I continued, "many of the ideas found their origin in Scotland and France. These ideas began to spread throughout Europe like an underground movement. The man who some call the 'Father of the Scottish Enlightenment' was named Francis Hutcheson."

"Wait," someone said. Your last name is Hutcheson! Is it the same spelling?"

"It is."

"Are you related to Francis?"

"I do not know. It would be an interesting connection if I were. In 1737, a fourteen-year-old boy began to study under Hutcheson, who was at that time the chair of Moral Philosophy at the University of Glasgow, Scotland. Hutcheson taught his young student enlightened concepts about morality, virtue, ethics, economics, and the true role of government."

"Who was his student?" asked someone from the back.

"His name was Adam Smith. Do any of you recognize the name?"

Heads shook in the negative.

Capitalism Vs. Socialism

"Adam Smith was Hutcheson's protégé. Smith would eventually succeed Hutcheson as Chair of Moral Philosophy at the University. At some point, long after Hutcheson had passed away, Smith began correspondence with a man named Thomas Paine. Smith rehearsed with Paine everything he had learned from Hutcheson, including two important beliefs Hutcheson is said to have strongly embraced before his death. The first belief was that the American colonies should be independent from England so the colonists can enjoy their right to 'life, liberty, and the pursuit of happiness.'"

The class looked shocked. "Are you saying that Thomas Jefferson didn't create that phrase?"

"That is what I am saying. Hutcheson schooled Adam Smith, who influenced Thomas Paine, *who* influenced Thomas Jefferson. You see it took many years and many great minds to distill out such a beautiful truth which ended up in the Declaration of Independence. Hutcheson was influenced by John Locke, Cicero, and others. So many great thinkers of the seventeenth and eighteenth centuries influenced the ideas expressed in the Declaration of Independence."

"Why haven't we heard of this before?"

"You would have learned about Adam Smith in college economics and about Thomas Paine in American History. We are just connecting the dots. In 1776, a big year in America, three documents were produced that affected the creation of America. Thomas Paine published an important pamphlet called *Common Sense.* In today's world it would be more like a political policy paper. That same year, Adam Smith published *The Wealth of Nations*. That book would become the most important book in modern economics. The reading of these two documents gave the Founding Fathers a great deal of comfort and intellectual support for independence. On July 4, 1776, a great moment in history, the Declaration of Independence was signed."

The class buzzed with excitement. "Wow! That's amazing!"

An astute inmate added, "I heard the Founding Fathers had once used or preferred 'life, liberty, and property.'"

"True," I said. "You see the phrase was used in that time in different ways depending on context and background. For example, on September 5, 1774, the colonies entered into the Articles of Association in which the phrase 'life, liberty, and property' was used. The articles were basically a contract among the colonies to join together to address grievances and intolerable acts of oppression by the King of England. The Articles provided the glue that held the colonies together during the fight for independence. It also sent notice to the King that the colonies would be ok discontinuing export of goods to England. It would also stop importing goods from England."

"I bet that got the attention of the King," said one.

"Oh yeah," said another.

"You know," said another, "The Articles of Association would be like if all inmates everywhere stopped working for prisons and jails for ten cents per hour. The prison would have to bring in lunch ladies, laundry workers, janitors, and repair crews from the outside. It would turn the economics of the prison upside down."

"Interesting example. However, understand I am not suggesting or advocating that you stop working.

Yet, I see you do understand the idea about the Articles of Association. It made the King realize he was vulnerable and rightly so. These documents influenced the founding of the United States, a place in which capitalism could flourish. You see, capitalism sprouts automatically, almost immediately, where liberty exists. The more liberty, the more effectively capitalism works, generally. The colonists were tired of being oppressed. Such oppression was devastating to their entrepreneurial pursuits.

"Generally?"

"Interesting that you caught that. Even Adam Smith realized that if moral virtue is absent in both buyer and seller, the risk of force or fraud exists. Smith called this truth 'The law of the Jungle'."[6]

"So what do we do if we have 'Law of the Jungle?'" asked another.

"Well, now we are back to balancing the intrusions of government to protect individuals who have been abused by those who refuse to follow two universal laws, which I will discuss next week."

"Guys," someone interrupted. "We just need to deal fairly and honestly and teach others to do the same. If everybody would do that, the need for government intervention would go away."

I smiled. "You understand. My work here today is finished. See you next week."

Week #4 Entrepreneurial Class - Principles of Behavior

The next week I asked my class, "well, any new thoughts that you may have had during the week?"

"Yeah," one volunteered. I've been thinking that if I had understood that I was putting a strain on the country, I probably wouldn't have done what I did."

"I am very happy to hear that. Now that you understand the principles, commit to follow them, and teach others to do the same. When we break the law, we cause our government to make more laws and make government bigger and nastier. It is like sticking it to ourselves. Any other thoughts?"

"We've been talking in the yard. Are capitalism and socialism opposites and at odds with each other?"

I replied, "well, it seems to be true, but not for the reasons that you might think. Capitalism is organic. It happens naturally within a free community or society. Socialism is like a genetically modified organism (GMO)." The class laughed. "Socialism is an artificial mix of government and a suppressed or limited form of capitalism. The academic definition of socialism is 'state-owned means of production, administration, and distribution.' In socialism, the nation or state owns the capital. What do you think the outcome is when socialism is employed?"

"It makes me think the economy is like a caged bird with clipped wings. If its wings are clipped, it can't fly."

Another added, "if capitalism is limited by government, people will not be able to get goods and services as easily."

Capitalism Vs. Socialism

"And the government will control our businesses through rules and taxes. It will take from us money to pay for things we might not agree with."

"Good thinking, class, excellent observations. Those who argue for socialism say that society has digressed to a point at which buyers and sellers can no longer trust each other to do business, which requires the government to step in."

A hand raised quickly. "Oh, I just had a thought. If capitalism is a natural occurrence, it must mean how God intends us to interact with each other."

Someone countered, "But what if people don't interact well with each other?"

"Well," I said, "it is at that point that capitalism breaks down. Capitalism is not the problem. People are the problem."

One guy added, "it's like the debate on guns. Guns are not the problem. People behaving badly is the problem. That is why government keeps trying to control guns. Then it can control the people."

"Being a citizen of the United States carries with it great expectations and implicit agreements with each other. The Constitution with its other founding documents and principles, presupposes that we will interact with each other properly and fairly. In other words, we must know correct principles and control ourselves."

Another student had a question. "I want to know how we choose a good government. And I want to know how politics could affect my chances of having a successful business."

"Well, let me explain. Politics is not always the same as regulation, but the two are always connected at some level to some degree."

Out of curiosity, I asked those who were democrats to raise their hands. A few raised their hands. Then I asked those who were republican to raise theirs. Again, a few raised their hands. But the overwhelming majority did not know with which ideology they closely identified. This class was going to be a very interesting meeting. I wanted to gauge their visceral gut responses to a few political ideas.

I first asked, "when you are a business owner, how would you feel if a federal agent went to your bank account and withdrew $2,000 each month and gave it to an employee of yours because the employee told the government that he needed it more than you...and there was nothing you could do about it?"

There was some discussion, but mostly outrage at the thought. Then I said, "what if that $2,000 is to pay for something that seems good, like medical bills or health insurance premiums?"

More discussion.

"What if the government told you with whom you had to do business?"

One inmate raised his hand and asked, "whatever happened to 'no shirt, no shoes, no service'?"

"My point exactly," I said. "What if the government told you that beach bums in sand laden shorts wanted to lounge in your five-star, coat and tie only, restaurant? Would it be right for the government to take your decision to serve or not to serve away from you?" The inmates were consternated over these possibilities.

"Whoa, I am simply the messenger. Do not shoot the messenger, okay?" We all laughed, and things calmed down.

"Okay, now let us talk about a woman's right to choose." All students shifted in their chairs, expressing a little discomfort on the topic. "Where does our right to choose come from? Does it come from the courts? Man's law? Man's authority?" There was a long thoughtful pause. "Or," I continued, "is there a higher authority than man's authority and a higher law than man's law?"

Someone asked, "Matt, are you saying that a higher power says it's okay for women to have abortions?"

"What do you think? Is it that what I am trying to say?"

One hand rose and the inmate spoke up, "I think what you are saying is that a higher Power—God—has given mankind the right to choose everything, including a right of a woman to have an abortion."

"Not exactly. It is much more complicated. I realize that it is a very touchy subject. I am not trying to persuade you in any direction. I only want you to begin to think differently so you can make up your own mind about your political leanings. This exercise is horizon broadening, okay?"

"Okay," they mumbled, looking at each other.

"If the Supreme Court confirmed only what a higher power had already conferred upon men and women, then why do we need any man-made laws at all?"

Seeing that question lost my audience, I clarified, "have abortion rates gone up or down since Roe vs. Wade?"

"What's Roe vs. Wade?" they asked.

"It was the Supreme Court's decision that gives women the right to decide what is right for them, including having an abortion, and clarified that the government should keep its nose out of our business between a woman and her doctor," I continued.

Someone made the comment, "It seems reasonable for the government to butt out. Since Republicans want the government to butt out, Republicans must really like that decision."

"Not so fast," I said, "there is more to it. You have heard of the Ten Commandments, right? The Ten Commandments are laws from God, and God said 'Thou shalt not kill.' So man's laws say it is legal, but God's laws say a person has moral agency to choose but must face the consequences of his or her decision to disregard God's law now or at a future time."

"Now back to the question. Since women know they can legally have an abortion, what have many of them chosen to do with their right to choose? What has happened to the numbers of abortions?"

"They've gone up," one inmate stated.

"Actually, they have gone down."

"So that's a good thing, right?"

"It means women are free to choose, and they are choosing NOT to abort more frequently."

Another inmate responded, "Interesting. Then why all the arguing about it?"

"Ah-ha. Now we are driving to the heart of the matter. What do the different political parties believe about abortion?" More shifting. Some smiles. Much anticipation. "I recommend you ask a friend or family member to send you a book called *Whatever Happened to Justice* by Richard Maybury."

Capitalism Vs. Socialism

"Who is Richard Maybury anyway?"

"He was a political-economic philosopher. Maybury's work will help you to find your political identity faster than I can. However, I will share a few true principles with you from his book. Maybury says that there are two basic laws that all human beings innately know to be true, and thus, are given by a Higher Authority. The first is 'Do all you have agreed to do.' That law includes implicit agreements with society such as do not sell illegal drugs or drive drunk. Society expects each of us to obey and honor this first law. The second law is 'Do not encroach on another's person or another person's property.'"

"What does encroach mean? You've used that term over and over, but I want to make sure I understand."

"It means to trespass, or to ignore the boundaries or rights of others."

"Understood."

"If you violate law #1 by driving drunk and crash into another car injuring or killing the occupants, you have encroached on another person's property. If you injure the passenger, you have also encroached on that person. Am I making sense?"

"Yes."

"So let us apply the two laws to the three scenarios I mentioned earlier. Which rule was broken when the government took $2,000 from you to give to your employee?"

"The second one...don't encroach."

Another hand sprang up and the inmate added, "Wait, isn't there an implicit agreement on Law #1 between you and your employee that you won't take each other's stuff?"

"Bingo, to both of you. Great job! But, what about the second scenario in which a business has to accept anyone no matter how he is dressed or how dirty and smelly he is."

Another man explained, "that beach bum had no right to ignore the rules of the establishment. He had an implicit agreement to honor the wishes of the restaurant owner. He also encroached by tracking sand all over and making the other customers feel uncomfortable."

"Excellent analysis. Now how about the last example concerning Roe vs. Wade. Think it through."

After silent pondering and deep reflection, one man raised his hand hesitantly. "There isn't a violation of an agreement unless the father wanted to keep the baby and the mother agreed, and then changed her mind without telling the father."

"That is certainly true with respect to an agreement between the man and the woman."

Another hand went up. There's no encroachment on the man because it is not his body."

"Thank you for those comments. Anyone else?" I asked.

No other hands went up. "This one is tricky," I explained. "What if an abortion encroaches on the unborn child's right to life, as stated in the Declaration of Independence? What if an abortion encroaches on the property (the unborn) or the agenda (bringing human life into existence) of a Higher Authority?"

"We hadn't thought of that. Encroaching on a Higher Authority?" The inmates considered and discussed this idea for a time amongst themselves.

"All right, guys, that is all for this week," I said.

"But wait," some said. "You never told us whether we lean Democrat or Republican."

You will have to discover that for yourself, based on these principles we have been discussing. Maybury has given us a framework to analyze our own actions and those of the political parties. But I will tell you, as Americans, we are closer in values and ideals than we think. If you think about it, all strife and contention in the world arises from the breaking of these simple laws. Now for you personally, society expects you to obey these laws. As long as you adhere to these laws, you will stay out of prison. The more thoughtful you are in obeying these laws, the more society will reward you. Remember: *Give, not take; Keep your word; Do not encroach!*"

Week #5 Documents of America's Founding

"Okay guys. Let us begin. We have had some good discussions thus far. We have learned that humans have a right to life, liberty, and the pursuit of happiness, unless they lose society's trust through bad behavior. We learned that capitalism is the natural, organic occurrence when liberty exists. Liberty yields capitalism. It is no more complex than that fact. Amassing volumes of academic studies will not yield a different conclusion. As Malcolm Gladwell observed in his book, *Blink*, 'all that extra information isn't actually an advantage at all; that, in fact, you need to know very little to find the underlying signature of a complex phenomenon.' All other economic and governmental philosophies are man-made to restrict liberty and free trade. They operate by fear or lack of moral virtue. We have learned that we can preserve capitalism and freedom by doing all we agreed to do and by not encroaching on others.

"Now, I would like to summarize the primary documents that were part of America's founding or greatly influenced it. You should read these documents at least once in your life. Better still is to study them."

September 5, 1774, Articles of Association

Early 1776, *Common Sense,* by Thomas Paine

1776, *Wealth of Nations,* by Adam Smith

July 4, 1776, *The Declaration of Independence,* by Thomas Jefferson

November 15, 1777, *Articles of Confederation,* agreed to by Congress; ratified by new states (formerly individual colonies). The new nation called the United States of America.

September 17, 1787, *The Constitution of the United States of America.*

December 15, 1791, *The Bill of Rights,* Amendments to the Constitution.

1795-2002, other amendments to the Constitution.

"It may seem like a lot of information, perhaps initially a little overwhelming, but everyone in this class, and every U.S. citizen, should read these documents. Those citizens of the world who are interested in America or who want to live in America, should also read them.

Will you read them?"

"We will," promised members of the class.

In the following weeks I saw various members of the class reading from these documents in the prison library. It made me so happy to see.

The Entrepreneurial Class concluded after a reasonably thorough discussion about accounting, economics, finance, business law, marketing, and organizational behavior. The experience was a good one, both for class members and for me. I hope in the future, these class members end up as productive citizens, living up to the principles they had learned. I hope the class will have played some role, large or small, in their future success.

As I left the classroom to return to my unit in the south yard, it was not lost upon me that eventually the members of that entrepreneur class would want to know if I had violated the laws which we had just discussed, which resulted in my incarceration.

Sure enough, within days several class members joined me on one of the many picnic tables in the south yard. As is customary in prison, they came right to the point.

"Are you a real believer of the principles you taught us the other day?" one asked.

"Of course," I said.

"But do you practice what you preach?"

"Do you think that I, a prisoner like you, should have some moral authority to teach those principles, that if I cannot live them, then I should not be encouraging you to live them?"

"Yeah, that's exactly the point."

"You make a good point, and I agree completely," I said.

"Does that mean you will keep teaching or quit?"

"Do you care what the answer is?"

"Yes, we really do."

"You want me to keep teaching the class?"

"We hope you will."

"Look guys, I was accused of making horrible mistakes which led to my incarceration. I did not do anything illegal. If I made any mistakes at all, it was due to my abnormal reaction to an abnormal situation. What happened to me is a complicated matter. I probably failed to communicate when I should have. I probably communicated too much when I should have been quiet. In the fog of war, many things went wrong at the same time. I was certainly overwhelmed and sometimes wondered what steps I should take next to correct what was going wrong. My honorable efforts to protect the investments were used against me, portraying my behavior as uncharacteristic. Many people who loved me and trusted me became confused. They had no idea what I was going through, and I could not tell them. They believed my behavior was indicative of wrongdoing."

"They think you were doing them dirty?" one asked.

I chuckled with a lump in my throat. "Yes, something like that. There were political undercurrents which I was fighting which I did not think I could share with them."

"You didn't think they would believe you?"

"You are correct. I certainly would not be any worse off if I had just told them everything. But at the time it was simply too difficult to explain."

"We understand, Bro. So you're not a mobster?"

I laughed. "No, no. I am definitely not."

"We know. Just kiddin.'"

"It is nearly impossible to change anchored beliefs. My friends, or former friends, or clients, or associates, will probably think I am a bad person to the day they die."

"Won't they forgive you? That makes them wrong too."

"Right now, they feel genuine betrayal. I did not purposely betray them, but what they feel is exactly the same as if I actually had betrayed them. It is a terribly painful emotion to experience. I do not hold it against them. I am hurting, too."

"Is there any way to fix everything?"

"I am trying...perhaps in the appeal."

"Hang in there, Bro."

We parted with the customary fist bump. Little did I know at that very moment, that I had already been betrayed by the attorney who had been appointed to handle my appeal. He did not intend to work on my appeal from the start.

A Final Word

Two Conversations

November 2019

A Final Thought on Capitalism v. Socialism

Matthew D. Hutcheson, known as Matt or Hutch, has helped thousands of federal prisoners discover socio-political truth. The following contemporaneous memorialization of an actual conversation gives a fascinating look into prison and prisoners, and what kinds of subjects are discussed on "the inside." Hutcheson memorialized dozens of such conversations and the following is one of them. This particular conversation happened in the Summer of 2015, before Matt was maliciously placed in solitary confinement for five months. (The Bureau of Prisons later apologized to him.) Matt presents ideas here that give an entirely new slant on why people should actually want to embrace capitalism over socialism in order to enhance their self-fulfillment. Better than a mere intellectual explanation about capitalism versus socialism, Hutcheson opens a window into his life and shares ideas that most have not previously considered. For whatever reason, young people today seem to be missing the most basic concepts about what makes America exceptional. In sharing these experiences from prison, Matt makes available desperately needed insight to millions. Many who know and advise Hutcheson felt it was time for these writings to become public. Every human being, wherever he or she lives on earth, should read, study, and ponder the deeply profound writings of Matthew D. Hutcheson.

Capitalism Vs. Socialism

Young Man: Hey Hutch, you believe in capitalism, don't you?

Me: Well, I observe it. It just is.

Young Man: What does that mean?

Me: Capitalism is not something that we merely believe in because we hope it is true. It is true because it is self-evident.

Young Man: Self-evident? I don't understand.

Me: Capitalism is not something that is created by man. It can only be discovered. Capitalism develops and grows spontaneously, like grass or wildflowers, unless of course, someone tries to destroy it by cutting it down or poisoning it.

Young Man: Umm, that isn't the answer I expected.

Me: What did you expect?

Young Man: I expected you to expound upon some philosophy. That's what you usually do when I ask you a question.

(Laughter)

Me: Capitalism has lifted billions of people out of poverty. Nothing except the Gospel of Jesus Christ has helped more people.

Young Man: Dude, I don't believe that. Capitalism has ruined my life and that of my family. I want socialism!

Me: Oh? How so?

Young Man: My skin is brown. Your skin is white. You have a ticket to success. I have a ticket to nowhere. I want socialism so I can finally get my share.

Me: Silence.

Capitalism Vs. Socialism

Young Man: Don't look at me like that! I am not the cause of the unfairness that exists in the world. It's capitalists like you that created all of the unfairness that exists today.

Me: Please forgive me. I was not looking at you in a disrespectful way. I was just thinking.

Young Man: About what?

Me: Why certain truths are self-evident to some, and invisible to others.

Young Man: Huh?

Me: Do you really think the color of your skin matters at all to a buyer of a brilliant product at a fair price?

Young Man: Man, what are you talkin' about?

Me: If you were to take my brain out of my head and place it on this table, and then take yours out and place it next to mine, no one would be able to tell which brain belonged to whom. Brains are brains. Outside of a head, they look the same no matter where you come from, what color your skin is, or what you believe.

Young Man: That is messed up.

Me: I am not trying to be funny. I am serious. Great ideas originate in the mind. Those ideas can be converted into products which people will purchase if they believe those products will make their lives better.

Young Man: That is easy for you to say. You are white.

Me: It is the words and ideas that come out of the mind that matter. Nothing else matters. Brown people all over the world invent new products every day. They have been doing it for thousands of years. Food, clothing, tools, intriguing inventions, etc.

Capitalism Vs. Socialism

Young Man: Yet they are still poor.

Me: True, many are. But it has to do with a lack of liberty, not skin color. Liberty can be "actual liberty" because it is established in the nation in which they live. Or liberty can be "perceived liberty" because an individual thinks he or she is free, or oppressed, when he or she is not. "For as a person thinks in his heart, so is he."

Young Man: Oh, come on! You are going to sit here and tell me my problems are all in my head?

Me: I am not diminishing one bit the difficulties you have had to face. What I am saying is that the pursuit of happiness and success requires capitalism. Socialism will suffocate what you hope to accomplish.

Young Man: Look, Hutch. I know that my people love you. All of them. That is cool. I just don't think you understand.

Me: I know what I have observed while I have been in prison. I have seen the unfairness and injustice. But it is not what we are talking about here. We are talking about your mind, and what can come out of it to make your life better, and also to make the lives of others better, too.

Young Man: I'm just tired of losing the battle.

Me: You do not really want something just given to you, do you? Easy street is what you want? What about self-respect? What about the joy of accomplishment and success following struggle and adversity?

Young Man: Now you sound like one of *those* guys.

Me: (Laughter) I know what you mean. What you need is a map. It is not that you cannot attain success. You simply do not have the map.

Capitalism Vs. Socialism

Young Man: There is a map?

Me: Well, not literally. The map is understanding some very important principles. You see, capitalism is not a form of government. Rather, it is a naturally occurring phenomena. The sun comes up, flowers grow. Capitalism is also that simple.

Young Man: The sun? I don't get it.

Me: It is metaphorical. The sun symbolizes liberty. Liberty rises, commerce and free trade thrive. If you have something good in your mind to offer, you will be rewarded.

Young Man: I'm confused. I think I must not understand what socialism is.

Me: Tell me your understanding of it.

Young Man: I don't know. It's the way of fairness. It's a way to make sure everyone has a chance. It's a way to prevent the rich from keeping us down.

Me: I do not want to put words in your mouth, but if I understand, you think socialism is some benevolent way of interacting with each other? You think it is a more virtuous, higher plane of living?

Young Man: Exactly! It is the next step forward in the evolution of our society! And the rich people are preventing it from happening because they are selfish and greedy!

Me: Do most people your age think and feel this way?

Young Man: All of them that I know.

Me: It is true that there are some "benign" forms of semi-socialism around the world. Denmark, the UK, Canada, or even Switzerland, have hybrid economies in which limited socialism and capitalism coexist. But they are rare. Even in countries like Denmark, there is so much regulation that a person would have to give up many freedoms to live there. Eventually, those people who are ok with it, adjust. Those who want to be free, leave.

Young Man: Benign semi-socialism is rare? What do you mean?

Me: Usually socialism becomes malignant. It spreads its tentacles into every aspect of a citizen's life until the citizen can no longer choose his or her own destiny. He or she can no longer pursue happiness.

Young Man: Pursue happiness? You mean, like, "the pursuit of happiness" from the Declaration of Independence?

Me: Correct. Fundamental to American belief is that our right to pursue happiness was given to us by God and that no man can take it from us unless we give it away or just let it go. Therein lies the danger.

Young Man: Danger? I don't follow.

Me: Once a people collectively lose or give up one right, the risk of losing others, or even all rights, increases rapidly.

Young Man: But you said Denmark and Switzerland make it work. They don't seem to be in danger.

Me: Those countries are the exceptions, not the rule. What usually happens is oppression. Take what we saw with the former USSR, or the "Union of Soviet *Socialist* Republics," or the DPRK, North Korea's "Democratic People's Republic of Korea," or China's "People's Republic of China." Those citizens are unable to pursue true happiness.

Young Man: North Korea's and China's names don't sound too bad. They have "People's" in their names.

Capitalism Vs. Socialism

Me: Using "People's" in the name of such a nation is merely euphemism.

Young Man: You-fuh-what?

Me: Euphemism. It means using a word to make a thing or situation sound better than it actually is.

Young Man: Oh.

Me: You see, the Nazis, Soviets, North Koreans, and the Chinese all have something in common. They have extinguished the individual's right to pursue happiness. Those governments utilized brutal control over their citizens, including taking away private property - a great source of happiness for many - and earnings from labor which resulted in individual poverty. They engaged in continuous surveillance, established concentration camps, tortured many, and committed executions without due process. The risk of flirting with socialism comes with the very real possibility of sliding down a slippery slope to misery.

Young Man: Those countries have not always been socialists?

Me: Not always. In fact, every one of them started out in an environment of capitalism. All nations do. Some do not understand the great gift that capitalism is: a gift from a Higher Authority, and they lose it by giving up their rights, one at a time, until misery and hopelessness result. It all begins with talk and ends in disaster.

Young Man: What does the pursuit of happiness have to do with capitalism?

Me: Everything, actually.

Young Man: How so?

Capitalism Vs. Socialism

Me: Let us talk about Hitler and the Nazis. Were they ahead of their time? Had Hitler and the Nazis reached this enlightened and benevolent plane of which you speak?

Young Man: Huh? What are you talkin' about?

Me: Tell me about the German Nazis.

Young Man: They were crazy people, evil people.

Me: What caused them to be crazy and evil?

Young Man: I don't know. They hated Jews and Blacks. They hated everyone except Germans.

Me: Did the Nazis hate others because of their race? Did their hatred begin and end there?

Young Man: Man, Hutch. You are killin' me. I don't know! What's your point?!

Me: I am not trying to frustrate you. I am trying to stimulate some deeper thought about the subject. The Nazis were primarily founded on economic ideas, not racial ones.

Young Man: Okay, so?

Me: Let me explain it this way...the official name of the Nazi party was the National *Socialist* German Workers' Party. NAZI was just an abbreviation.

Young Man: (Silence)

Me: The Nazis, or socialists, placed the government over the economy, over the right of its citizens to pursue happiness. It placed the government over medicine, research, production of food, music and the arts, the news, entertainment, transportation, and more.

Young Man: (Silence)

Capitalism Vs. Socialism

Me: I have heard you making music. Socialism means an end to that. If a socialistic government wants you to make music, it will tell you what kind of music to make. Perhaps polka. How would you like that?

Young Man: What the...that's crazy! I'd hate that!

Me: How do you think Jay-Z and Beyoncé would feel about being told they could no longer make music? Under socialism, Jay-Z may be driving a cement truck, because the government dictates what its citizens do. Under socialism, the government controls the capital. Whoever controls the capital, controls what is produced, how its production is administered, and how the product or service is distributed. Under socialism, Beyoncé may be told to make shoes or cut meat in a butcher shop. How do you think she would feel about it? What a waste of the gift within her!

Young Man: (Silence)

Me: Would Beyoncé be happy or sad if she could no longer pursue what she loves to do?

Young Man: Sad.

Me: Capitalism makes it possible for her to pursue her dreams, to pursue happiness. You see, socialism is not enlightenment. It is oppression. It is a violation of two fundamental laws that all people everywhere know to be true.

Young Man: Two laws?

Me: Yes. The first law is, "do all you agree to do," which includes implicit agreements. The second law is, "do not encroach on another person or another person's property."

Young Man: I don't understand. What is an implicit agreement?

Me: Do you remember the Declaration of Independence?

Young Man: Well, I know what it is, but I have never read it.

Me: "We hold these truths to be self-evident (naturally occurring or naturally obvious), that all men are created equal, that they are endowed by their Creator with certain unalienable Rights, that among these are Life, Liberty, and the Pursuit of Happiness."

Young Man: Right. I remember.

Me: "We the People" implicitly agree with each other (first law) to protect the right of all other citizens to pursue happiness.

In other words, an implicit agreement is one that is so obvious between two or more individuals that no one can argue with it, even if it is not written down in a contract or other formal agreement.

Young Man: Such as?

Me: Well, for example, when you earn a driver's license, you implicitly agree with all other citizens that you will not drive drunk, so you do not hurt them. All holders of a driver's license implicitly agree to do the same.

Young Man: That actually makes sense!

Me: The most important implicit agreement understood by all Americans - or at least should be understood - is that we agree to protect each other's rights from the encroachment of others, including ourselves and the government. It is how we remain free.

Young Man: Whoa, this is all starting to have an effect on me. This conversation is starting to change my thinking.

Me: What is happening is that you are discovering something that has always been there. Truth is that way. Our Founding Fathers described truth as "self-evident." It is naturally occurring. Man does not create truth. He can only discover it.

Young Man: (Shaking his head with a huge smile, having *discovered* a life changing reality.)

Me: There is one other thing I want to share with you.

Young Man: Okay, go ahead.

Me: The early European settlers of America wanted to control their own destiny and make their own decisions even if it were more difficult or less predictable than having a "king" who dictated the course of their lives. Those settlers thrived on individual initiative, hard work, and freedom of choice.

Young Man: Yeah, they thrived on the backs of slaves.

Me: We can have a discussion about slavery another day. But for now, can we finish tackling the socialism versus capitalism topic?

Young Man: Sure.

Me: Although the early settlers could not at that time define what they wanted for their lives in academic terms, but they could feel an innate drive within them to attain every human potentiality. They wanted to activate every capacity within them. The King of England was preventing that aspiration.

Young Man: Just like they later did with slaves.

Me: I know slavery is a sore subject, and I promise we will have the opportunity to discuss it soon. But for now, please let me explain some very important truths, okay?

Young Man: Okay.

Me: It was not until 1943 when Psychologist, Abraham Maslow, theorized a "Hierarchy of Human Needs," which explained the innate drive within them. His research paper was called "A Theory of Human Motivation."

Young Man: I've heard of Maslow.

Me: Excellent. He explained that the basic human need is food, shelter, and clothing; physiological needs. Then, safety from danger caused by man or beast. Then, love and belonging to a family or tribe. Then, respect of friends and community. Finally, self-actualization.

Young Man: What is self-actualization?

Me: It is the "attainment of one's full potential" and the "activation of all a person's capacities." That particular definition of self-actualization was developed by a famous psychologist named Carl Rogers, who has long since passed away.

Young Man: I like that thought...the thought to activate all of my potential.

Me: Yes, me too, and you will need capitalism to do it. Without capitalism, you will be prevented from going past the point of earning the respect of family and community.

Young Man: So, you are saying that if Beyoncé is forced to work in a butcher shop, she will be unable to fulfill the potential within her, which would limit the community esteem she would have otherwise enjoyed.

She would not be the magnificent self-actualized entertainer she is today, and that would limit her pursuit and attainment of happiness?

Me: Precisely. Capitalism made Beyoncé and all others like her possible.

Young Man: I see.

Me: Think of Beyoncé and socialism as I quote Winston Churchill, the UK's heroic World War II Prime Minister, *"Socialism is a philosophy of failure, the creed of ignorance, and the gospel of envy. Its inherent virtue is the equal sharing of misery."*

Young Man: Beyoncé would be miserable if she could not express what is in her. I can see how socialism would prevent that expression and the attainment of her self-actualization.

Me: Self-actualization is possible for you, too. But it will not be if Americans embrace and operate at a lower plane of interaction, one that is based on restriction, not liberty. You will be able to achieve only so much. That is socialism and socialism violates the implicit rule that all Americans have entered into with each other: Protect the right to pursue happiness and do not encroach on another person's right to obtain it.

Young Man: This conversation has changed my life.

Me: I am glad.

Big Second Conversation

This second conversation occurred in 2017 at FCI - Lompoc, California. The conversation was between Matthew D. Hutcheson and an immigrant in the United States illegally. Hutcheson is respected within the United States prison system by inmates and staff alike.

Capitalism Vs. Socialism

This respect uniquely affords him the opportunity to have frank and candid conversations about very sensitive subjects with inmates which would otherwise be virtually impossible in any other setting. Hutcheson's love and respect for these men comes through clearly.

. . . . .

Hispanic Man: Hutch, my brothers asked me to speak to you.

Me: *Como esta usted, hermano? Todo bien?*

Hispanic Man: *Todo bien, gracias!*

Me: *Hablame.*

Hispanic Man: I don't want you to be angry with me. It seems like every time I try to discuss this with an American it ends up in an argument.

 Me: Discuss what?

Hispanic Man: Promise me this will be a respectful conversation.

Me: *Lo prometo.*

Hispanic Man: *Gracias*. Why does Donald Trump hate Mexicans or anyone with dark skin for that matter?

Me: I know the media tries to portray him that way, but I do not think he hates anyone.

Hispanic Man: It sure sounds like he hates us. It sounds like many Americans hate us, too.

Me: Americans do not hate you. They simply do not like that you do not respect the two universal laws.

Hispanic Man: Universal laws? I don't know what those are.

Me: You innately know. Every human being does.

Hispanic Man: What is innately?

Me: It means you understand without someone having to tell you. The knowledge or understanding simply is in you.

Hispanic Man: *Entiendo*.

Me: Here is the real issue, and it has nothing to do with your skin color. It has to do with breaking both laws, laws that Americans deeply value and respect, when someone sneaks into the United States illegally.

Hispanic Man: What are the two laws?

Me: The first law is, "Do everything you agree to do," which includes keeping implicit agreements. The second law is, "Do not encroach on another person or his property."

Hispanic Man: What is an implicit agreement?

Me: It is an agreement which honorable people make out of basic human decency and respect. For example, if you cook a meal for me in your restaurant, we have an implicit agreement that I will pay you for that meal.

Hispanic Man: *Ah, ya veo!*

Me: When someone enters the United States illegally, he or she breaks both laws. Americans do not like these violations.

Hispanic Man: *Entiendo*.

Me: Disrespect for the two universal laws demonstrates to American citizens that the violator does not understand something that Americans hold to be self-evident. Self-evident means: obvious, it goes without saying, or naturally occurring.

Hispanic Man: This has never been explained to me. *Por favor continua*.

Me: All nations have laws, including boundaries. China, Russia, or even Canada for that matter, will not allow you into their country just because you want to enter. They, too, want to know that you respect the two laws. Nations have implicit agreements, or perhaps even written treaties between them, stating that citizens of one country will not try to illegally sneak into the other. It is frowned upon everywhere, not just in the United States.

Hispanic Man: *Ok, ya veo*.

Me: So, a person breaks the first law when he or she disregards the implicit agreement or immigration treaties between nations. By breaking the first law, he or she encroaches on the people of that country.

Hispanic Man: What does encroach mean?

Me: It means *traspasar*; to trespass. When one encroaches, he or she violates another person's space, property, assets, peace of mind, happiness, etc. He or she receives benefit from services paid for by American taxpayers without paying taxes themselves. Thus, it is viewed as theft of labor, investment, and tax revenue by the American people.

Hispanic Man: (Listening)

Me: While inside the United States you receive protections from police, the United States Armed Forces, direct economic benefits, and even the Constitution itself, yet you do not respect the laws that make those protections possible.

Hispanic Man: *Entiendo*.

Capitalism Vs. Socialism

Me: It does not matter what color a person's skin is. Americans do not like violators of the two laws. Do you now understand why?

Hispanic Man: *Ya veo.*

Me: On the other hand, Americans love those who obey the two laws. If someone obeys law number one by entering the United States legally, Americans really respect him or her. It is those individuals who are celebrated and given help. It is those who are not likely to break law number two just like regular American citizens.

Hispanic Man: Well why didn't someone just explain that to us? That makes perfect sense to me. We value the United States just like you do. We want to live in the United States.

Me: No, that statement is not true. You do not value the United States. We are a nation of laws. If you truly valued the United States, you would first value and obey the two laws. We do not want violators of the two laws living here because we cannot be certain you have our backs.

Hispanic Man: *Que quieras decir?*

Me: What I am saying is that fundamental to being an American citizen is an implicit expectation that we have among ourselves to protect the rights of others. It is the reason our Constitution is so powerful. It is the reason America is so powerful. We do not let people, or even our government, encroach (law #2) on our fellow citizens. In fact, our government's primary purpose is to ensure that no one or nothing encroaches on the rights of its citizens.

Hispanic Man: (Listening)

Capitalism Vs. Socialism

Me: Because you broke the two laws when you illegally came into the United States, we cannot trust that you to have our backs. How can we know that you will protect our rights if you disrespect the laws that exist to protect those rights?

Hispanic Man: *Ya veo. Nunca avia pensando en eso antes. Lo siento.*

Me: *Gracias por decir eso.* We want you here if we know for sure you will obey the two laws. It all starts with obeying them in the first place. Skin color has absolutely nothing to do with it.

Hispanic Man: Yes, I see that now. This conversation has really helped me to understand.

Me: Will you teach your brothers these things and ask them to teach their families?

Hispanic Man: *Por supuesto.*

Me: *Gracias hermano. Buenas noches.*

AUTHOR

Matthew D. Hutcheson advocates for those who do not have a voice. His advocacy favorably impacts the lives of over seventy million Americans, including investment transparency, prison reform, race relations, jobs creation in struggling economies, affordable health care access, and uniting those of varying cultures, religions, and political persuasions. A Seattle native, he is blessed with a beautiful wife and four children.

"Socialism is responsible for the deaths of more than 100 million victims."

https://www.heritage.org/progressivism/commentary/what-americans-must-know-about-socialism

AreULost Press
For more information:
info@areulost.org

Psalm 82: 3-4

Defend the weak and the fatherless;
uphold the cause of the poor and the oppressed.
Rescue the weak and the needy;
deliver them from the hand of the wicked.

***

Other titles at **AreULost** Press available at Amazon:

Quinny by Matt Hutcheson

Worshipper Warrior by Steve Holt (Under Worshiper Warrior Press)

God Wild Marriage – 2nd Edition by Steve Holt (Under Worshiper Warrior Press)

Little Lamb by Jan Inman

Titles by Jay Inman

Perspicacity: Book 3 of the Culling

Walking at the Top of the World: Book 2 of the Culling

Black Gladius: Book 1 of the Culling

Varangian Guard

Canticle of the Magios

Sunigin – Book 1 of Circle of Deception

Insurgio - Book 2 of Circle of Deception

Certo - Book 3 of Circle of Deception

www.ingramcontent.com/pod-product-compliance
Lightning Source LLC
Chambersburg PA
CBHW051233250726

48655CB00006B/2748